Red
Redeems

Poetry and Prose
Inspired by God

Karen J Chisholm

Red
Redeems

Poetry and Prose
Inspired by God

KAREN J CHISHOLM

Inks and Bindings
888-290-5218
www.inksandbindings.com
orders@inksandbindings.com

Books by Karen J Chisholm

I AM with You
Poems Inspired by God

Tough as Nails
Poems Inspired by God

Voices
Poems Inspired by God

In Green Pastures
Poems Inspired by God

This Book is Dedicated

To the Glory of God

It could change your life!

Contents

Foreword

*"So teach us to number our days
that we may apply our hearts unto
wisdom."* Psalm 90:12

Lord, You gave me joy in my salvation.
You gave me hope in Jesus Christ. I shall
appear before Your throne when my days on
Earth are completed. I will worship You.
I shall have eyes to see and ears to hear.
I will see God.

In daily life, I forget your commands. The
world is so present and You seem so future.
Speak to me again this morning. Encourage
me in my faith. Remind me of the promises
You have made to me. I want to rejoice and
sing and worship You today. I need You.

*Child, I AM ever with you. I AM as close as
your breath. Do not fear. You will not forget
to include Me in your thoughts and actions,
for I AM with you. You woke up thankful
today, just as you did yesterday.*

*Do not fear sins of omission, for I AM with you.
Speak My Name. I AM. Tell Me who you are,
whose you are, what you will become.*

I am the righteousness of Christ displayed
for all the world to see in all my faults and
imperfections so that the miracle of salvation
in my life is made clear, giving others hope
for their own salvation.

I am an epistle written by God, full of words like "I love you" and "I want you anyway" and "You are Mine." I live to glorify God by carrying in me both the dying of this world and eternal life that shall be revealed. I Am a Promise that you made to Yourself.

I belong to Christ.
He redeemed me along with all mankind: whosoever will. I am bought with the blood of the Lamb slain from the foundation of the world. Before I was lost, I was saved by Holy Sacrifice. Before I was, I am His. And now that I am, I serve Him for the sheer joy of it, because I love Him who is Love.

Every, only, any, all. Those are the sum total of people allowed to come to Jesus for salvation.

It does not yet appear what I will become because when I see Him, I will be like Him. Just like Him: Holy. Eternal. Love. All the fruit of the Spirit. The fulfilled promise of the ages standing before the throne of God, worshipping I AM with my whole being! All that I am is Him. Miracle of God with hands and feet, and a heart that is His.

FOR-EV-ER !!!

Section 1

God Speaking

Red Redeems

There's never been a perfect man
Until I walked this earth.
And only once in stable dark
Was there a virgin birth.

Long planned and spoke in heaven
Finally came to be.
That holy night in Bethlehem
When truth was born to see.

Long foretold a savior came
'Twas God come down to man.
I came to bring you life from God,
Fulfilled the Father's plan.

And it would take a miracle
For God to walk the Earth.
I came to show His mercy, love,
Bring Grace: believers worth.

I watched and waited 'til the time
Came round the circling years
And Satan tried to turn men's minds
With power, bringing fear.

And all the years I was a child
He tried to stop God's plan.
Once thrown from heaven,
Threatened bold, he couldn't touch I AM.

When 30 years were satisfied,
My life he sought in vain.
As My disciples saw it all,
Grace touched lives like rain.

I knew My time was coming soon.
I taught disciples truth.
They couldn't understand but saw
The healings I would do.

Those with Me in the garden slept
While I was laying down
The miracles, the healings too
Like leaves upon the ground.

And as I walked away as just
A humbled sacrifice,
Was emptied on Golgotha's hill.
For all, I paid sin's price.

The blood that flowed from Calvary
Is seen in heaven now.
For every soul My blood has washed
Is born again even now.

My disciples spread the Word
Still going forth today
That whosoever will may come
To rise redeemed to say:

I am redeemed by
The Blood of the Lamb of God
Through the holy blood of Jesus.
For you see . . . Red Redeems.

My Son

Beloved, eternal
Sent here by God
Lent to earth for a span
Sent for salvation
Discipled the twelve
Christ, Son of God, son of man.

Born of a virgin with heralding star,
Sought by the wise and the meek.
Healed and did miracles
Taught of the kingdom
Here is the One whom you seek.

Jesus the Christ
Long-awaited Messiah
Plain, everyday-looking man
Tender and loving
Inflexible, strong,
Obedient to death: Father's plan

Walked on the water
And wept for his friend
All things were in his control
Died on the cross
From the tomb raised to life
He lives, so you live, are made whole.

Sing of God's Love
For the hopeless, the lost,
His offer to save all from hell.
Write of His Presence,
The Peace He delivers
The grace that you walk in as well.

Come meet the Savior
Who knows all you've done,
Who loves you in spite of yourself.
Standing before you
He offers his hand
"Come try me, I AM, your soul's help."

Why not today?
The question is offered
Tomorrow's not promised to any.
Will you deny him
Or hold out your hand?
You, chosen one out of many.

I would
That you meet
My Son.

Genesis

Awe inspiring, elaborate Plan
Laid down by God Who created man.
Spoke into darkness, the face of the void,
"Let there be light," and the darkness deployed.

Time was begun with the sun and the moon,
Great light and lesser light, stars untold strewn.
The sea brought forth creatures of water domain.
The earth brought forth animals, both wild and tame.

Man was created in My own likeness,
Was given My nature, both anger and kindness,
Was given dominion to rule in the Earth,
Was fitted with feelings of sadness and mirth.

Whatever he wanted he did with great strength.
He walked, jumped, stretched, lifted,
Could run any length.
He didn't know he was made to connect
'Til I used his rib to make Eve while he slept.

Together they came, met with Me in the cool.
Each evening at sunset we walked near a pool.
Adam learned much in this Holy reverie
With Eve, his helpmate. They learned from Me.

Then came the sly one in serpent form
"Did God really say?" started the storm.
But they had been trained in the cool of the day
When blocked from the Garden,
Could make their own way.

They learned when they stumbled
And, hungry, they found
Food I had planted that sprang from the ground.
They still turned their eyes to the Garden, to Me
In the cool of the evening, wherever they'd be.

And so the first prayers gave them comfort
And helped as they lived, raised a family,
Like the animals, whelped.
And they always remembered their Maker in this:
The God of all Glory began Genesis.

I AM . . .

I AM Glorious, I AM ever
None has seen My Face
Call to all folks everywhere
Found in every place

Every gender, every age
All the human race
Are Mine, belong to Me
Can be redeemed because I AM . . .

Some serve other masters
And don't believe I'm real
They find it inconvenient
To know a God who heals

Prefer life in control
Results come out their way
Deny they had an option
When they face Judgment Day

I AM Holy, I AM God
My ways past finding out
Yet I dwell here with men
My words come from their mouth

I sent My Word to heal them
They feel in self they're strong
They're mine, belong to Me
But choose their right, their wrong

The young ones …they all know Me
But in their growing up
The tutor of experience
May lead to bitter cup

I AM God eternal
I have always been
I know all men's hearts,
AM here to be their Friend

Love unconditional is Mine,
Offered here for free
And anyone can find me,
Become, belong to Me

Others too may find Me
Are thankful to be caught
Many come to heaven
Not hell where fire is hot

Soul salvation
   Brings fresh joy
     All Mine . . .
        Belong to Me

I AM

My Grace

This is the day I have made just for you,
All of you blessed of the Lord.
This is the day I would speak to you, too,
By My Word which is called Spirit's sword.

Holy and Righteous and true to My Word,
I keep every Promise I've made.
All that has come since Adam you've heard
Of My people on pages is laid.

All of My chosen My love and wrath feel.
This is My Testament: I Am the Lamb.
This is their history; they are My zeal.
For I AM . . . that I AM.

I have allowed them to go their own way
But do not think they are unloved.
I'll never leave them or turn them away.
I guide with My eye from above.

The Gentiles are offered to know Me as well.
I've broken down partition's wall.
There at the cross where I defeated hell.
I gave My life once for all.

Now, whosoever seeks Me will find
I'm no respecter, won't judge.
Those who are searching with repentant mind
Learn I forgive all, hold no grudge.

Any lost soul may approach, may come near.
I welcome those with trembling hands.
They are My heart, are especially dear,
For they come without guile . . . to I AM.

I'm no respecter of person or skin;
I have redeemed all mankind.
I do not measure the depth of man's sin.
There *is* no one righteous to find.

And to sinful man is extended My aid:
Whosoever will may come.
I died just once and sin's debt is paid.
Through Me, the Gate's wide: all, not some.

I will not change you; no, you'll change yourself
When you see now that you are forgiven.
I will reveal, too, Who I AM Myself.
You've never known Love that's grace-driven.

I want the unruly, the lost and the cursed.
Test Me and try Me and bring Me your worst.
Though men reject you, with Me you come first.

Prove Me wrong.
Bring it on
Til you come . . .
To I AM.

Accepted

Forgiven. Remission. Translated
Into the Kingdom of My Dear Son
The Son of My Love.
Heaven's Love Child. Dear.

His Life is very dear,
Laid down by an act of His will
In obedience to My will for you,
For all who believe.

In Him you have new life.
You have been brought out of darkness,
The darkness of this world, into His Light.
The Light of Heaven shines in your heart.

You have been translated
From darkness to light,
Out of lies and into truth,
Bought with the price of Holy Blood

Shed only once.
Offered freely to be received freely
By those who could never
Redeem themselves.

Even if mankind could offer their own blood,
Their own lives, it would not make them holy,
For they are not holy until Christ's blood
Covers their sin and makes them holy.

In heaven only the shed blood of Jesus,
God's Son, is acceptable.

And now those made holy by believing
Jesus Messiah died in their place,
Have asked Him to live in their hearts,
And know His Word.

By Spirit's revelation of Truth,
Men laid down their lives,
Were witnesses . . .
Martyred for their testimony.

Their blood is precious to Me.
Their sacrifice is sweet to Me.
Their love is perfect and
I keep them close to Me.

They cry from under the throne
For salvation completeness
For those souls their witness speaks to.
They pray for you.

Intercession continues in heaven,
Christ interceding for believers, and
Martyrs interceding for the lost ones
Who may yet come to Christ.

All men want their lives to count.
All want to leave a legacy,
To be remembered,
For their lives to have mattered.

Child, your life matters.
Because Christ lives in you,
You are Mine.

Continue in My Love,
Hid with Christ in Me.
I AM Love.

Now turn your eyes to Me.
Know that I hear your prayers.
Your praise glorifies Me.

Your songs are sweet offerings
Out of your thankful heart,
Speaking the truth you have learned.
Beautiful.

All who read this, sing to Me,
Then sing yet more,
For you too are beloved, My own,
Perfect in Christ, whose sacrifice
Avails for sin . . . forever.

And you need only call My name
  In faith, believing I hear you,
    And you will be covered
      By His blood . . .
        Accepted.

Crushed

Here we are, Me holding you
Broken and dying, yet becoming new.
This, My calling, reserved for a few,
Has come. And you . . . are crushed.

When you were younger, you laughed and you ran.
You didn't think twice on the calling of man,
To serve in God's kingdom, His salvation plan
Until now. And you are . . . crushed.

Had it together, all things in control.
Worried? No, never! You met every goal.
You lived without knowing you were not whole
'Til I came. And you . . . were crushed.

Blame, accusation, and tears were your bread.
You stumbled as blinded, could not see ahead.
Your life was in ruins, all numb as if dead.
Then I came . . . to one . . . I'd crushed.

Slow, halting steps though the rubble, you came.
Lifted your head when I called you by name.
Grabbed for the rope titled 'Hope' that remains
As you came . . . to the One . . . Who'd crushed.

Why-me questions unanswered remained,
Ignored as if nothing was asked or retained.
But Love supported, surrounded the pained
One who hurt . . . who lay there . . . crushed.

My Son was crushed, too. He even died.
Tried in the crucible, alone and denied.
Bought back the sinners from serpent that lied
And He lives . . . the One . . . life crushed.

Now you have realized Love covers all.
You've received joyfully, deeply, God's Call.
Turned over your life, with new purpose stand tall
And you see . . . you had to be . . . crushed.

Long years now past and I'm still in your heart.
Humble, you serve Me, will do any part.
With joy you draw water salvation wells art
You are glad . . 'twas by Me . . you were crushed.

Today you are different: less manipulation.
Today you are humble: complete transformation.
Today you are speaking to each tribe and nation:
Come see . . .
    You go free . . .
        When you're crushed.

Do Not Judge

Continue in the faith and do not judge.
There are those who pull away,
Seduced or persuaded
Or mind cruelly tricked, taken.

You do not know whether
You would do better in their place.
Each will answer for their own words, actions.
Each is loved unconditionally.

Some martyrs finish their race swiftly . .
With blood.
Others come through long years
Of subtle torture of the mind,
Reduced in the end to apostasy.

Do not judge.
You have not walked their path.

I AM with them to the end,
And beyond, into My Presence.
A life cannot be compared to another's life.
Only I know. I AM merciful.

Do not expect to leave this life
Without having your faith tested,
Beaten down, questioned, weighed,
For you, too, will fall short.

That is why I came.
Every living soul stands in need of a Savior.
You focus on Me, only on Me
And by Grace . . . you *will* be saved.

You

You are; yet you aren't.
Seen, yet not seen.
Nothing, all, everything:
What these words mean.

Born from within,
Ever will be.
Flesh and yet spirit
Placed here by Me.

Knowing intuitively
Things you've not learned.
Trusting unseen,
Hearing, you've turned.

Trusting 'tis My voice,
You've written words My own,
Prayed for unnumbered,
And sung words unknown.

Space is a mystery
You move in each day.
Can't separate from Me.
Oft do what I say.

Even not knowing
'Tis My plan for you,
Done My will often.
My thoughts come through you.

More open you are to Me,
More you receive.
Even denying Me,
Still you believe.

Else why the fear?
Why the what-if, the fight?
It's hard work to go
'Gainst the flow of My might.

And yet I have granted
Your choice in it all.
Believe I exist here
And answer My call,

Or choose other deity,
Worship and serve.
Pleasing yourself or
Another takes nerve.

Each god believed in
Is there in your heart.
I see it all clearly.
Of you, I'm a part.

The potter imbues deep
The pot with himself.
And many can see it plain,
Even on shelf,

I'm in My creation,
Each part and each piece.
It's proven by microscope,
Studies released.

And so when you serve
Other gods, you will find
There's tension because
I Am there in your mind.

Your DNA proves that your
Genes are from Me.
You agree with yourself
When you worship Me free.

Your Father I Am
Have been so since came Eve
From rib I created,
Completed both, pleased.

Mankind bears My image
Upon every atom.
It's always been so,
Ever since Adam.

Deny you may try
But it won't satisfy.
You'll find when you die,
You are Mine.

Father's Discipline

Always I AM Love.
Discipline is for your good,
Meted out in mercy.
It isn't even My first choice;
I prefer the carrot to the stick.
I woo you and bless you
And carry you when I must.

The work of the cross not only
Made you a way to come to Me,
It changed *everything*.
Now I can come to you, and you'll live.

I made rules in the beginning
So we could have relationship:
God-to-man; man-to-God.
From of old, only a single man at a time
Who turned over his life to Me
Could approach the holy,
And that with blood.

You see, man does not comprehend holy,
Has no reference point
Cannot see what is unseen yet present.
So, it was too easy for mankind
To cross a line and trespass the holy.
Once *anything* trespasses the holy, it dies.
There must be blood to even approach.

It is no different today.
There must be blood.
The shed blood of Christ
Is continually in My Presence,
Fulfilling the requirement for all.

This blood still lives.
It is alive forevermore.
Dead blood brings death.
Only living blood brings life.

And no blood is not an option,
For blood is required.
If there is no blood sacrifice,
The one who approaches
Forfeits his own blood.

You want to know why blood is required.
Blood is life. You think breath means life,
But without blood, there can be no breath.
One cannot work without the other,
Cannot remain in existence
Without the other.
Breath is Spirit and Spirit is God.

I give every living being life
And when one dies,
Their spirit returns to Me.
I AM the living God.

And you are made in My image.
No, I do not look like you;
You look like Me: Alive.

Come to Jesus and live.

Flawed on Purpose

Child, you are Mine. You will always be Mine.
Those words don't make you cry anymore.
Your tears of repentance washed your heart
You've healed In ways you didn't know you were hurt
And My love covers you as a garment of grace.
My peace stays with you everywhere you are.

When you get upset,
You always remember to look to Me
And connect to My peace again
Just as I've taught you to do.
One thing you still do I'll address here again.
Stop finding fault: You're you.

I am pleased how I made you:
Imperfect on purpose.
How else would you ever have need
To seek out a savior or long for my heaven
Without mankind's fall through sin's deeds?

The worse you repine for what you've done,
The more grace abounds and forgives.
The more you then value my Son's sacrifice,
His shed blood: By faith, You then live.

My purpose unfolds and will surely come
To its planned end in your life.
Together with those gone before and come after,
You will all glorify Me.

In heaven you'll tell how My grace and My mercy
Defeated My foe, made you free by Christ's blood.
Flawed on purpose. I made you this way
So no one could boast saying "Look at me!"
"I saved myself and I don't need God."
In vain Jesus died on the cross, then, you see.

So sin in the now brings Me glory and laud
My Kingdom grows as the broken seek God.
And my enemy who thought he'd be equal to me
Is defeated by loathed, despised souls set free.

And I laugh!
I laugh with sheer joy and deep love
Over every flawed human made My tool of grace
By the shed Blood of Jesus Christ to win souls.

The more flawed you are,
The better I can use you in My Kingdom.
The more I can show forth My grace in you,
The better I like it.
That's why whosoever will may come."

Flawed on purpose. Yes!
        Flawed on purpose! Mine!

Grace

Grace to redeem you, to bring you to Me:
Powerful Grace long foretold.
Grace that sustains you, keeps your spirit free
And claims you as sheep of My fold.

Every misstep and wrong action and word
Could, under Law, cost your life.
Grace suffers long and with patience awaits
Covering until time is right.

Even those living on dregs I AM calling.
Keeping you breathing 'til time of your change.
Watching and waiting, I stand at heart's door,
Ready to give you new life that remains.

Promise I'm with you unseen and unknown,
Grace brings My blessings on all equally.
Unmerited favor, this Grace I have shown;
On the just and unjust, Grace is free.

I'm calling to you now, "Child, come unto Me,"
I'm longing that you seek My face.
I want you to know Me as I well know you,
Showering you with My Grace.

Spirit is drawing you closer in time to
The day you must fall to your knees.
Each one must come to the end of their rope;
Grace then connects you with Me.

You're free to choose to know Me or not.
This is your chance to believe.
Those who give over their life to My care,
New life in Christ will receive.

Chance after chance after chance
Brought to you . . . by Grace.

I Have Found a Ransom

I have found a ransom!
One who sins not
One who resists not
One who protests not
I have found a ransom!

I looked among men
To and fro my eye sought
And I found not one
Who did only my words
Who did only my will
Who had only my heart

And my only Son
My heart
My soul
My life
Said I will go
I will do
I will say what you say
I am here

So long I had asked
Who will go for me?
Who will speak my words?
And do my will?
Who will walk in truth
My way only?
Who will go?
Who will go?

Many heard my call and volunteered
Many ran the course
But because they were not me

And man had no remorse
Fleeting was redemption, temporary . . .
Sin regained dominion
And I looked again.

Time and again
Sin and redemption
Cycle and circle
Never resolved . . .

I have found a Ransom . . .
I am here!

Planned? Yes, it was.
I saw it, created it,
Set it in motion.
I spoke of it often,
Offering hope.

Knowing the end
Kept my wrath many times
Seeing sin finished,
I helped man to climb

To finish his course
Each one free to choose
Knowing the answer
Not willing to lose . . . a one

I found the answer! In myself, In my own
For my love is filled up
My creation complete
As I watch it play out
I can wait . . . for I found the answer!
I have found a Ransom!

I'm Hiring

The field of harvest is white and full
All while crop waiting, more hands are needed.
The laborers many, still more to come;
Souls gone, unknowing, who would have
heeded.

I paint the sky with sunsets daily
Message in clouds that cross the sky
My Love forever will fail them never
But they don't know Me, and some will die.

I am hiring now and paying wages
To whosoever would work My fields,
To tell the lost ones My love for them,
Snatch them from hell fire: My glory yield.

There is a tempter who is deception,
He paints the Savior as just a man.
He scoffs at Grace, says none need saving,
Knows he won't win, keeps who he can.

The work is hard, unthankful, treacherous,
I need more workers, I need more hires.
And you'll be fishing for the lives of men,
Pay delayed; benefits won't expire.

So come today; answer the call;
Think not your skill has part to play.
I'll take who will come, take any, all;
It's OJT, yes, all the way.

And you can do this right where you are.
Some will want details, some shut you down.
Just talk to people, good news impart
And trade your smile for their cold frown.

The ones who're hurting are ready now.
Just picture yourself there in their place.
Offer to pray then, no skill, and no how
Just simply urgent, come seek My face.

Then, while you're praying, be thankful too.
Any can come, need not be lost.
Speak of your Savior; give them a clue,
Tell how He died there on the cross.

Ask Me to save those they love most;
You pray with passion to intercede.
Ask Me remember and save these souls
When you plead for their great need.

Now who will take this opportunity
And who will answer by word or act,
Be hired by God, set others free?
Let him step forward, enter My pact.

I AM with you wherever you go.
I save the souls, whether now or later.
I give the words that you don't know.
Those words remembered, they'll call on
Savior.

Now, let's talk wages.

Section 2

God Speaking

Lover of My Soul

In the deepest part of living things
The Spirit lives and thrives.
For those who seek eternal wings,
See life through spirit eyes.

And if the spirit there is dark,
How dark that life will be.
No room for Christ or patience for
God things that eyes can't see.

Life's toll peels back the layers and
A glimpse of Light revealed
Can make a difference in a heart
That once was cold and steeled.

Jesus, lover of my soul,
Has knocked on inner door.
A little Light can show the key
To heart closed off before.

And darkened spirit, cold and starved,
Has choice to let Him in.
For if invited, He will dwell,
Will cleanse that heart of sin.

The Light grows stronger yet to see
The darkened soul made clean.
New life in Christ begins make sense,
Brings hope 'stead broken dream.

New life unknown is offered now
To spirit, soul, new heart.
Rebirth can always be retraced
To Light embraced at start.

The Lover of My Soul came for,
Redeemed the souls called man.
To please the Father, right the wrong,
The only One who can.

His work is done, His life laid down
To buy back souls of men.
Transaction sealed in heav'n by blood,
He took it up again.

Now grace at work in every life
Buys time to find the way
To answer knock at heart's door where
Dark turns bright as day.

Grace covers all, the dark, the light,
And even those between.
Steady, always, Love of God
Is drawing souls, unseen.

But some dark souls refuse the light
Because despise, reject
God's goodness, see it as a fake;
The life they know has their respect.

They love the darkness, love their sin,
Embrace not keeping rules.
Wist not this world is backdrop, stage,
Are gladly Satan's tools.

Their one mistake is thinking their
Allegiance is returned.
By this world's prince whose only goal
Be God since heaven spurned.

He wants to rule all things, always
To have it all his way.
And men are grunts he uses, dupes
In darkness he can sway.

The prince of this world offers power,
Makes promises untrue.
And lies of dreams of power beyond
What's known by me and you.

Unknown by followers, he won't share
For long his power with men.
It's too much fun receive their praise,
Know their eternal end.

But all the while God's Spirit draws
And promises new life.
Eternal kind where hearts submitted
Rule with Him, no strife.

And Jesus, Lover of My soul
Is King of kings and Lord.
When the day you hear His knock,
Answer quick: Light poured

On you.

    Real Life.

Let Him Come

Let him come to me . . .

If I thirst, unsatisfied,
I remember words You cried,
Loudly offered all who'd come
Slake their thirst in God the Son.

When I'm thirsty, as I drink
I remember these words, think
What an offer You have made!
"Let him come" by Son we're bade.

Just as Father bids us come,
Invitation same as Son's:
Everlasting covenant
God's sure mercies, heaven sent.

If we're looking, we will find
God loves seekers; love is kind.
Overlooking obvious flaws
Because Son fulfilled His laws.

I am thankful I can come
To the Father through the Son.
I am needy; I have cares.
I need help and answered prayers.

I am thirsty, I would drink
I need saving from the brink.
I believe and cleave and trust.
Rely on Christ as sure I must.

Living water freely flows
Inner fountain. How? God knows.
I am filled with Holy truth
Spilling forth in words that sooth.

Offering hope I have inside
Trusting hard when faith is tried.
"Let him come," you said. I did.
Following after like a kid.

Help me, show me what to do.
Living water comes from You.
It spills out from inner me,
This belly-fountain full and free.

Because . . .
                    . . . I come.

On Faith

Any size faith is powerful.
It's faith that connects you to God.
It speaks of believing and knows that God is.
In you before birth, faith unflawed.

Faith will be tested and put on display,
Tried by the enemy somehow each day.
Wearingly worked on, but can't be snuffed out,
This faith eternal, fathomless, shouts:

God's will be done whatever the reason!
Still, faith prays on through every life season.
"Glory to God!" come the words on the lips
From believer, unmoved, wading life's little slips.

Faith is man's constant connection to God.
The helmet o'er breastplate on one with feet shod
With Gospel of Jesus, God's Son sent to die,
Redeeming all men from the enemy's lie.

Nothing can separate one who believes.
Death on the cross brought them life's reprieve.
Jesus, the Way to the Father on high
Sits on right hand, intercedes while men try.

Faith is eternal, cannot fade away.
For Spirit-sealed souls, the Lord will display.
"I paid the full ransom and this one believed."
The crown handed over, Son places, received

By head-bowed believer so thankful for grace,
Amazed to be with Him, held in His embrace.
Faith cannot shatter, be lost or misused,
Cannot be denied when with hope it is fused.

Faith doesn't bow, break, get dented or sore.
It's steady at all times when fear comes to fore.
It's patient and calm when all hell breaks loose.
When fear drains away, it remains, still in use.

Never forget you have faith you can call on.
It's strong without reason, still there with the dawn.
'Fore you bowed your head, asked Jesus come in
To live in your heart and forgive all your sin . . .

Faith was there.

One

One Offering
Perfect Sacrifice
Once for all
Redeemed.

Opened the door
All can come in
Blessed be
Our God.

Standing alone
Bearing all sin
Rejected, bruised,
And bleeding.

Christ's blood atoned,
Souls be made one,
Stands now for us
Interceding.

Glory to God
Great One in Three
Honored obedience
Was offered.

Blood of the Lamb
Slain from foundation
Once on God's Altar
Was proffered.

Ordered aright
Follow the word
Our steps and His
Hand in hand.

Here is the deal
God's love is real.
Heaven has come
Down to man.

Those who are seeking
Will find way to God
Whosoever will
May come

Then be transformed
Darkness to Light
Following closely
God's Son.

Jesus, Redeemer
Who waited in time
Comes back to Father
God's will complete.

Open arms waiting,
All may come in.
Come sons and
Daughters once flawed.

Once are redeemed,
Turn, share glad story.
Others will
Want to know more.

Those who believe
At once born again
Those who won't listen,
Ignore.

All have a chance to
Come here, to know Him.
Spirit draws souls;
Holy chore.

Delight of the Father
All honor and praise
Belongs to the
Great Three-in-One.

Never too bad,
Too far, or too late
If you are still breathing,
Then come!

God is pure Love.
He wants you to know Him.
Made perfect way
You can come.

Nothing withstanding
God's perfect love
Walk in the Light
Of the Son.

So, come.

Playing

You think you are just playing?
Your words are life and death.
Misunderstood by gunman,
Can lead to your last breath.

Misunderstood by friend
Brings tension into play.
Rejected by a foe,
Can make this a bad day.

Words build up or they tear down.
Inflection can be key.
Delivered loud with threats or soft
Still literal they be.

Your words are so significant
Even passing time of day,
You're speaking life or death to self
By what of self you say.

Oh, I was kidding! I'm just playing!
But denial shouts
Oops! I didn't mean to say
What I thought out loud.

We toss out words that others take
To heart quite literally
And treat these words like coins we toss
In wishing fountain free.

Words last longer than even pennies.
Though we can't recall
Just what we said to who or when,
God's angel wrote them all.

So when you're feeling playful,
Try to keep it about you.
Don't joke and laugh others' expense
Because your words are true.

Most likely, if you joke like that,
Because it's what you're used to.
You learned to play with words this way
When they were said of you.

The thing about playing is,
You don't do it alone.
Playing requires two or more
Unless you are a clone.

And being funny gains you "points,"
Small measures of respect.
So when you're "on a roll," you speak
Wit-words you'd not inspect.

Words can build and can tear down
Because they set in motion.
Words create, they bring to pass
Events you'd had no notion.

If you speak your dreams aloud
And often, picturing,
And take the necessary steps,
To life these things you'll bring.

So playing words are just for fun
But they'll bring forth a harvest.
Just make it what's your favorite.
You'll eat them, even sharpest.

Keep your playing positive
And say just what you mean,
But say it so it liberates.
Don't say words rude and mean.

Whatever words you sow come back
To haunt or make you glad.
So while you're having fun with friends,
Speak words of life love-clad.

Here's a hint:
If you can't think
Of anything to say,
There's a reason for that.

Keep quiet.

Self

Why do you justify self by another,
Building up self at expense of a brother?
When you find fault and pronounce he is bad,
Does that make you good then?
O that is so sad.

It's like if you focus on bad deeds he's done,
You justify self; it makes you the good one.
You don't have to face it;
You don't have to change.
While condemning his actions,
You stop at self-blame.

But there is a nature in man God calls sin.
Self-realization; comes standard within.
Each, every newborn demands its own way.
In the terrible twos, No! their favorite word say.

All of your life really, you're your own god
Whether corrected or dad spared the rod.
But, child, I still love you however you act.
I know this sin nature, and that is a fact.

Here in the world you choose life trajectory
The angel the soul takes: Is it lifted to Me?
Will you love darkness rather than light?
Or will you love Truth more than the lie?

If you won't listen when you are reproved
Or yield in the crucible, refuse to be moved,
Deny God in heaven, deny God's own Son,
What have you gained? What have you won?

Life is the testing ground. Will you choose light?
Yielding your own, seeking the right?
Agree you're a sinner who can't save yourself,
In need of a Savior? You know there's a hell.

Because you were taught, trained while still young,
You learned of sin nature that fights 'til it's won.
Selfish and focused on running own life,
This nature would dominate others, cause strife.

You cannot change you and get it to stick.
Intentions soon fail when your mind's like a brick.
Determined to get your own way all the time,
You're really embarrassed; your motives all find.

Manipulation's a sad way to live:
Planning on getting, a little you'll give.
When all goes your way, on top of the world.
Then, when it doesn't, react with lip curled.

Only redemption can stop this cascade.
Foot of the cross must be where life is laid.
There, when you die to the god that is "me,"
There put on Christ, you will finally see . . .

It's not about you.
This life . . .
Is about . . .
Jesus.

And what do you get out of it?

Peace.

Unforsaken

Steady steps made sure by Christ
Take me toward the Son.
Who'll go with me to His side?
Those His path begun.

Unforsaken, bought by blood of
Heaven's perfect Lamb:
Never lost or set aside,
Each child of Great I AM.

Father's promise "I AM with you"
Comforts us with grace.
Sin o'ertakes us, yet He makes us
Want to seek His face.

What's the draw? It's that we're wanted.
All who will may come.
When we're given grace to seek Him,
New life's then begun.

You ask me why I care so much,
For He died long ago.
I say because it's not who you are.
It's really who you know.

It's Who knows you enough to love
Before you're ever born,
Enough to put up with your stuff,
To love all those who scorn.

You see, He was forsaken once
On Calvary long ago,
Hung on a cross to pay the cost
Of sin so all could know

Redemption from the Fall of man.
He died to save the world.
And promised man salvation from
This place we're tossed and hurled.

God's Word says He created evil.
That news bothered me
Until He opened up my eyes
And I began to see.

There's nothing good without the bad.
It's yin and yang and balance.
Without it, we would have no choice,
Could value no one's talents.

We'd have no hope and no remorse,
No hero/villain novel.
And I'm not sure we'd even care.
There'd be no need to grovel.

The wisdom of Creator God
Put tension in the world
When Lucifer the light bearer
From heaven to earth was hurled.

He chose to be a deity,
Wanted to be God.
He got a throne through cold deceit,
A place he's run roughshod.

Adam and Eve became game pieces
In this power struggle.
Renamed Satan, he made sure
Got all the souls he'd smuggled.

His reign, just like his victory,
Is full of darkness, sin.
His question, "Did God really say?"
Men still can hear within.

He makes it seem we give up much
When we convert to Christ.
A trade of dark for light occurs.
We see we've been enticed.

All this time, we've bought the lie
That God's forsaken man.
Daily further we're reduced.
We're pawns in Satan's plan.

But Father God, Who's only Love,
Knows there will come a day
In each one's life who lives below
When we'll meet with The Way.

His name is Jesus, the Messiah.
He has come for you.
The Good News is, He rose from death
And in Him you will too.

He beat the devil, saved the world,
And paid the price for all.
Forsaken on the cross that day,
Redeemed man from The Fall.

Now He reveals the Father's plan
Shows He's already won.
And we in Him can rise up too
With resurrected Son

To live . . . Unforsaken.

What Will You Do?

You have to be lost to be found
To be drowning or dying to be saved
You have to want help
To reach out for a hand
Needing a Savior who's brave.

When you've lost all hope
Are resigned to the worst
Living a lie, know you're under the curse
Know there is One
Who's the last and the first
Who will save.

He hears when you cry
He will answer your call.
When you're too pooped to try,
Catches you when you fall,
Can restore what is lost,
Cannot be reclaimed.
And His name?
Jesus

When you're living a lie
That all's right with your world
When life brings hard punches
And bitter words hurled

When you're down for the count
And you lay there tight curled
He's the One.
God's own Son.
Jesus.

You cannot be saved
If you don't need a savior.
Get by on your cunning
While currying favor.

Your house made of cards
Not yet trembling at all
You haven't an interest
In Adam, the Fall.

Then He calls.
     Through your walls.
        Jesus.

Former and latter, beginning and end
Alpha, Omega,
True seeker's best friend,
Rescues the sinner
Who's come to rope's end.
To seal.
     He's real.
        Jesus.

Have you considered
Why you've turned him down?
Avoided and sidestepped
Or met with a frown.

Held your ground.
     Stepped around.
        Jesus?

He's patiently waiting
To show you the way.
He listens and watches
O'er you every day.

He hears other's whispers,
Your sins He would pay.
Will you pray?
Today?
Jesus.

What is sin?
Why the onus?
I hear you exclaim.
No one's better than other
You say in disdain.

Not ready for Bible,
That old ball and chain.
You maintain
I'm insane.
Still there's Jesus.

What will you do about it?

Who Knows You

It's not who you are or who you know,
It's Who knows you.
He knows you can't be good enough.
He knows—He always knew.

And so the Lamb of God was sent,
Slain from the world's foundation.
This Lamb, God's Son, came as a man:
Simple—no reputation.

How many songs and stories told,
Spoke, sung in verse and rhyme?
How many Bibles have been sold
Throughout just one lifetime?

He's King of kings and Lord of lords
But came here a babe.
He walked the dust and wiped the sweat,
On simple folk hands laid.

Nothing to prove, no need to boast,
He came here for one thing:
To die in agony and pain
To save the world, was slain.

He taught disciples who would tell,
He promised Comforter
Who'd lead to truth and give them words
That no man can confer.

God's Holy Spirit still leads those
Who love the Lord and listen.
He knows those who've sold out to
The Son of God Who's risen.

If you have spent time on your knees
With Jesus in your heart,
You know the soundless voice of God,
His Holy Spirit's part.

And if you won't deny He speaks,
He'll lead you into truth.
Not who you know but Who knows you,
Will cause you to bear fruit.

And Spirit fruit is wonderful!
It's love and joy and peace.
Makes waiting here so bearable
Brings others comfort, ease.

God brings surprises every morn
Trials and joys, it's true.
It's not who you are or who you know,
It's only Who knows you.

Motives

Where do they come from,
Fighting and wars?
Somebody somewhere
Is kicking down doors

They're not getting quick enough
What they've got coming
So take what they want
By treachery and cunning.

Others ask God
But then fail to receive.
They ask with wrong motives,
Or don't yet believe.

Unfaithful to God
To be the world's friend
Thus makes God their enemy.
What is their end?

Meanwhile, God's Spirit
Is jealous with Love,
Yearning for welcome
In us from above.

He gives holy power
To prevent life stumble;
Resisting the proud,
Gives more grace to the humble.

Be subject to God
Resisting the devil
Stand firm; watch him flee,
Keeping self on the level.

Come close to God
And He'll come close to you.
Wash your hands and stop wavering,
With pure heart, pull through.

Repent, even weep
O'er your disloyalty.
Feel shame for your sins
And grieve what you see.

Humble yourselves,
In His Presence, feel small,
And He'll lift you up,
For the humble stand tall.

Don't even think of
Criticizing a brother.
You're judging the Law
Passing sentence on other.

There is but One
Who is able to save.
With life and death power
He conquered the grave.

Come now you people
Who plan to make money,
Carry on business,
A year where life's sunny.

You have no clue
What may happen tomorrow.
Your life is a vapor
Disappearing in sorrow.

Instead, you should say
If the Lord wills, we'll live
And do this or that
In the time He may give.

As it is, you are boasting
In your self-conceit.
Such boasting is useless,
Leads to self-defeat.

So, any who knows
What is right but won't do it
Sins against God and self
All the way through it.

Check out your motives,
Tell me, are they hidden?
If they won't stand the light
Then the devil has bidden.

What can change a heart?
A motive?
Only God's Spirit, Christ's Blood,
Self devotive.

So what can be done
With a life that's like mine?
Come to the Cross
Though I stumble, repine

Receive Your forgiveness
Be honest with sin.
I'll take your hand
Your new life begin.

Thank You

Thank you for Your Spirit!
What a glorious gift You've given!
Thanking You opens me
To things of God in heaven.

Thank you, Jesus, Son of God.
You gave Your life for all;
Obedient One, God's Holy Son,
Redeemed us from The Fall.

And gave gifts to men,
To whosoever will may come
You give water of Life freely
Drawn from salvation's well.

And gave gifts to mankind,
Whoever would could come.
You gave water of life freely
To all, not just to some.

Bringing us to God,
Reconciling us to Him,
Freeing us from doubt,
From worry, death, and sin.

We focus on You and live.
Thank you.

Arrested

I stand arrested, stopped in my tracks.
Though not repenting, still I look back.
Hearing the cries of the people I've robbed,
I see I'm a sinner. I'm wanted by God.

While I am standing, I turn and look back,
Seeing through God's eyes my life and my lack.
Consider this filthy road I'm walking on,
See there is better; to light I am drawn.

Whatever it takes, He has paid to redeem.
This race He created, sin fallen, made clean.
And I am partaker in the nature of God.
I've asked Him come into my life, once a fraud.

My world is changing. Gone the old plan.
I've met the Christ and I'm a new man.
Bought with a price, redeemed by His blood,
A trickle, a ripple, a torrent, a flood.

I've used other people; I've made it my aim,
Defrauded, abused their trust for my own gain.
And nothing and no one could get through my web
Or stop the full, headlong plunge by my greed fed.

'Til I was arrested and shown how it felt being
Duped, robbed, molested, tricked, left with no help.
I kept on in trespass, in sin against those
The weak, unsuspecting, the simple I chose.

Now I'm their champion, I help where I can.
I've been born again and I'm a new man.
The old man has died who used others for fun.
I spot ones like me a mile off, make them run.

I work for the Lord now. I'm led by the Spirit.
I walk in the truth and the light; I don't fear it.
With nothing to hide, I look men in the eye
And I have all I need; I've found God will supply.

Arrested by God was the best thing could happen.
Dead in my trespass and sin, I was nappin'
In truth I was hurting myself by my actions,
Would never grow up or mature by a fraction.

God opened my eyes to my sin's consequence
On the ones that I love who love me, no pretense.
And I finally saw who I was, what I did.
Had to stop, stand, and face up the fact I'm no kid.

So now I help others. I reach all I can
To tell them of Jesus, God come down to man.
The great Mediator who paid for man's sin,
The strait gate to God for all who'll come in.

Whosoever will may come
Be arrested.

Deity

God
Always right
Inflexible regarding truth
But truth in love
Brings pain that heals
The sin that bleeds the soul

Obedience
To the Father's will
May also seem inflexible
But truth in love
Will show in time
The trap that was avoided

Grace
Redirects
Along the path of Life
That comes from God
Allows to make
Another, better choice

Mercy
Love in purest form
Withholds death deserved
Stands sentinel and waits
In wrath remembers love
To the final breath

Truth
Revealed by Spirit
Stands up to will
And won't be moved
Or gainsaid by logic

Jesus
Creator
Redeemer
Mediator and Advocate
Alone trumped death
And lives

Salvation
By belief is knowing
Jesus Messiah
Is the Gate
To new life now
And then forever
Amen.

Section 3

God Speaking

Crucifixion Judged

You saw a movie just last week.
The Passion of the Christ.
You'd not believe they'd show such gore
On TV Sunday nights.

"Unnecessarily cruel," you said,
Those stripes on Jesus' back.
Whip cuts that bought your healing,
Paid it all—with nothing slack.

You think exaggeration,
But you weren't there that day.
Not standing by to hear each lash,
Not splattered by the spray.

You didn't hear them pound the nails
Nor see the sword pierce through His side.
You didn't chant word "Crucify!"
Would that Christ had neater died.

You were not present on that mount
To see night wipe out day
Or hear the thunder like a shout
Nor feel the earthquake sway.

You never viewed the faces there,
The ones who thought they'd won.
Or hopeless, helpless followers
Grieving o'er God's Son.

You didn't hurl one insult then;
You weren't around to tell.
But still today you judge it for
Strong language, violence, hell.

Go back to your safe modern home.
On Sunday watch your sports.
And hope don't find yourself in need
Or child's life threat'ning short.

What happened on the cross that day
Was not a little thing.
Holy God offered His Son;
He sacrificed Heaven's King.

He bought you back,
Those sold in sin.
He ransomed slaves
Just ordinary men.

And when the God who made the stars
Does something so immense,
He doesn't spare not detail one.
You bet it's too intense.

For some of God's great miracles
Have been made seen of man.
Witnessed, reported, then passed down.
E'en that's minutely planned.

And when you meet your Maker
And you see His glory cloud,
Remember *all* is necessary.
Be thankful He allowed

You. . .
    To *know*. . .
        Such mercy.

Perspective

Find no fault with one I find holy.
Make no plan to change or make amends.
Trust My blood is enough to cover.
Expect to see Me in your final end.

There's no matter rough regret can change.
Penitence will never overcome.
Only grace will lead to life salvation.
All come short; You're not the only one.

Forge ahead. Take strides away from sin.
Keep coming. My arms are under you.
Look higher. Your help comes from the Lord.
Go deeper. You'll find My Word your truth.

Step surely. I will keep your feet on path.
Trade sorrow for joy. I'm holding tight.
Then linger. I would show you just a glimpse
My Glory. Know the cross will end the fight

Inside you. Where you think you can't be free,
My Word stands, reminds you I AM All.
Stop looking at self and look to Me,
Your comfort—every time you fall.

I AM your righteousness.

So, Come

Holy, Perfect, approached here with blood,
Whosoever will may come.
Christ has torn down all walls of partition,
Race, color, creed, it is done.

There is no distance, excuse, blot or stain
That forever between us can stand.
The shed blood of Jesus continues, remains
And the Gate now stands open to man.

So come.

Come as you are: broken, bleeding, disdained,
Aloof, clean or dirty, or covered with sores,
Deb, stud, or heathen, rich, poor, free, or chained,
I'll take you all, make room for more.

I've sent invitations, and message in stone,
The stars, trees, and wind call your name.
My Grace covers all and Christ's blood still atones.
I take all your sins, scars, and stains.

You're why I came.
        My Love remains.
                So, come . . .

All things are ready; there's room yet for more.
Compel men to come to the feast.
I've blessings to spare and rewards set in store;
Come quickly south, north, west, and east.

Tremendous in power, My strength can command.
All things bow obeisance to Me.
I've given freely My Spirit to man;
Each one chooses, for I made you free

To choose.   So, come.

The time fast approaches when choices are gone.
The day of the Lord draweth nigh
When no man will work or discern right or wrong;
Mountains will melt, black the sky.

Trouble not seen will envelop the earth;
Men will cry out everywhere.
Cut off, the sound of men's laughter and mirth,
The Earth where you lived will be bare.

His kingdom in ruins, the Prince of this world
Having nothing to reign o'er in power,
With nothing to show in his hand tightly curled,
Will have spent here his last, final hour.

And when he is cast into the fiery lake
That forever will belch smoke and burn,
All those he deceived, every soul he could take,
Will go with him to never return.

Those who have called on my name, I have kept,
Each soul who cried out, saved and tried.
Every man, boy and girl, every woman who wept
For sheer joy, I'll have here at My side.

I'll never lose a one.

So come.

That I AM

Over and over,
And over again,
Foot up foot down,
Foot up foot down.

Walking with Jesus means
You just keep going.

Foot up, foot down,
Foot up, foot down.

No matter what comes,
You hold to My hand.
When the storm passes,
In Christ you stand.
Lost on life's ocean,
I bring you to sand
And you know . . .
That I AM.

Every believer
Redeemed from The Fall
Came through the fire,
The storm, flood and all.
Though you're bowed low,
In Christ you stand tall
And you know . . . That I AM.

Every connection
To Me is God-made.
All of creation:
Each rose, rock, and blade,
All serving Me,
They do as they're bade
And they know . . . That I AM.

I came as a man
In the fullness of time.
I walked on the earth
To fulfill God's design.
I prayed in the Garden
"Your will, not mine,"
For I know . . . That I AM.

Once resurrected,
Appearing to men,
I showed and I proved
From beginning to end
I AM who I said I was:
One God would send
So all know . . . That I AM.

Now life's star players
Are people like you,
Ones who've surrendered
To the Way and the Truth.

Who follow the Spirit
And bid you do too
So you know . . .
That I AM.

Yes, you know . . . That I AM.

The Cost

Few often listen when I speak of the cost.
They know of My dying and My resurrection.
They read what is written, how My life was lost
And some may make surface connection.

I am revealing Myself to you.
You too must die to be raised.
There is a way to come deeper in Me
Living this way brings deep praise.

Seven and twelve, fifty and forty:
Numbers as symbols you know.
The pivot is one, the basis, the goal,
The deepest place in God you'll go.

Counting the cost of abandon to God
Scares many people away.
Dying to live comes at great cost
To really *know* I am The Way.

Your time in prayer, time spent waiting on God
Requires a big chunk of your time.
Rising 'fore sunrise and reading My Word,
Searching . . . your life hid in Mine.

Would you consider, come deeper in Me?
Spirit is wooing you now.
Counting the cost of narrowing your world,
You'll be pressed hard to learn how.

It isn't the time or the doing or prayer
That makes this expensive to learn.
It's what you give up, what choose to let go
That changes how your spirit yearns.

You have the gifts to do a great many things,
So many, your time seems to scatter.
But if you would master, do this one thing well,
Focus and time are what matter.

Your God spot becomes dojo;
You do as you're told,
Obeying without thinking why.
And little by little, line upon line,
Precept on precept, time flies.

Your worth in the world and relationships suffer;
You must submit to your Master.
This is the pearl of great price at great cost
Known by God, title you're after.

Your God spot becomes dojo;
You do as you're told,
Obeying without thinking why.
And little by little, line upon line,
Precept on precept, time flies.

Your worth in the world and relationships suffer;
You must submit to your Master.
This is the pearl of great price at great cost
Known by God, title you're after.

It only takes everything:
Focus, time
Time, focus
And paying the cost
With your life
The way
I did.

Warrior

All you have gone through in life to this moment
I used here in shaping for Me.
Made you for a purpose that fits with My plan;
Knew that this day you'd be free.

Free of the bondage of pleasing and pride.
Free of the works of your hands.
Come through life's fire well battered and scarred.
Here in My will you now stand.

You can accept now and rest in My love
Or, grudge held, accuse Me, not care.
This choice, freely offered, is given to all.
Whosoever, My life can share.

I paid the price, I bought the world back.
Dominion is now Mine to rule.
If you don't believe, I Am still King,
The deceiver'd like keep you his tool.

I paid the price of redemption for all,
For every human who ever lived.
But I Am the God who forgives and forgets,
I bring you through and love give.

My men are warriors in spirit
In battles unmanned and unseen,
Enforcing authority given to them,
Standing for God/man between.

That is My place of authority:
Still captives I'm freeing today.
I Am their Lord and their leader and so
Prayer warriors go where I say.

There are no wimps in My army.
I fight their battles, 'tis true.
They walk in freedom from bondage.
Can I say that about you?

The thing is, you have to believe it,
Embrace all I did on the cross.
Spend time in My Presence awaiting
So I'll know you well: You're no loss.

Come to Me just as I've made you:
Angry and mad and footsore.
You will find faith, peace, and healing,
Discover new life I've in store

For you
   Today,
      Now,
         Forever.
           Come.

Like Jesus

Forgive.
It's too hard to carry around
The weight of unforgiveness.

Bless.
Go beyond letting go of anger.
Move into wanting good for them.

Love.
Desire them to know Me.
Treat them as if they already do.

Trust.
Roll all your pain on Me and let go of it.
Believe I connected your lives at this time,
In this way, for a reason.

Receive
The full blessing of heaven
For loving your enemies.

Move on
Into joy. When you love unconditionally,
You are allowing Me to shine through you.

Let go.
Allow Me to draw them to Myself
My way, in My time.
They have a better chance of salvation
With your forgiveness and trust.

Expect.
Talk to Me about them not to complain,
But to speak of what will be for them
When their darkness is shattered by My Light,
When the Morning Star arises in their soul.

Receive
Every blessing for being Me to the one
Who tore and snatched at your peace.

Remember.
I forgave those who crucified Me,
Asking Father to forgive them
For they didn't know what they were doing.

Do not judge.
It does not yet appear what they shall be.
Your soul was once in darkness as theirs is now.
Today may be the day of their release.

Pray
My will be done in earth as it is in heaven.
You may be the key to their forever life.

Believe
I AM a rewarder of those who seek Me.
See them saved and serving Me
Out of love, with thanksgiving.

Start.
Today is the day of salvation for someone.
Why not the very one who hurt you?

Let go.
I will work in their life. Only I can save them.
This is My doing.
I brought you into their life for such a time as this.

Follow Me.
Let go of pain. Don't rehearse it.
Don't preserve it in your memory.
Let it go and follow Me.

After all,
The next person who will hurt you
Is waiting.

Make Him Run

The memories that stab you
Are not brought to you by Christ,
Spirit not reminding you of sin.
Father threw them far away,
Remembers not against you.
A brand new start when you were born again.

So, when will you stop hurting,
Then repent in humbling prayer?
Again and then again you ask in vain.
That sin has been removed,
Washed clean,
Forever pardoned.
Christ bore your penalty,
Yet guilt remains.

The accuser of the brethren
Is at work to keep you down.
His time is short; he's doing all he can.
To keep your peace off-kilter,
Discredit Christ the Lord,
Claim even the redeemed of fallen man.

He lulls you with distractions,
Then questions if you're saved
Because you jump each time he brings up sin.
Pick up your shield of faith.
Remember Whose you are.
Pull out your sword and say the words again.

"No weapon formed against me shall prosper,
Having done all, I stand
And quench the fiery darts against me hurled.
My righteousness is in Christ
He paid redemption's price
My life's in Him who overcame the world."

Now take your feet in gospel shoes
And plant them on his back.
Jump up and down; remind him of his fate.
For you have full authority;
Just stand and watch him run.
His time is short and God is never late.

So, make him run,
Then watch Me smile.
There's nothing I won't do for those who stand.
With eyes on Christ Who is the Prize
He conquered *for* you and
It's just the way I planned.

Remember who you are.
Remember Who I AM.
Remember you're redeemed by God's own Son.
Stand tall because you're Mine.
Don't let the dark take over.
Just speak the Word and watch the devil run.

Yes, make him run!
    I love, through you,
        To make him run!

Nothing Between

Nothing can come between you and your Savior.
Sin cannot; good cannot; nothing between.
You live in God in unmerited favor.
In heaven, your rightness in Christ only seen.

It's like I'm wearing rose-colored glasses.
I see you perfect, unspotted, and clean.
Viewed through the blood of the Lamb slain for all,
Only your faith in Christ Jesus is seen.

Nothing can stick to you; nothing remains
Of all the sin in you, rife.
Here in His Glory, no blemish retains.
King of kings, Lord of lords gives you life.

Nothing means nothing. There is no argument.
The accuser has nothing on you.
It's his word against My Word,
No matter what's seen,
You're born again, clean and new.

So, when those words come to you,
Saying you're bad, things like
Awful, ashamed, wish I were dead,
You substitute "God so loved this whole world
That He gave his Son Jesus" instead.

Then go on: "Jesus' blood paid the price for my sin;
He was wounded for My transgressions.
Chastised for my peace; all my sins laid on Him.
'He is Lord' has become my confession."

Your blue days will scatter, My light shine within,
And the weight of your sin will have flown.
My Peace satisfies you and you will walk on
Hand in hand with this Savior you've known.

Nothing between you and your Savior,
Make sure there is nothing between.
Don't fall asleep until you are clear
With the One Who lives in you unseen.

Nothing means nothing.
    Let nothing between.

Others' Offenses

Many's the time you have judged for yourself
Situation seen with own eyes.
Words said against you, comments that stung
Caused so-called hackles to rise.

Other times witnessed unjust words against
Ones who meant something to you.
You were right there and you heard it all,
Know and report it for true.

Now, you must trust your friends, stand up for them;
There's no reason they'd fabricate lies.
But sometimes the telling includes how they felt.
You weren't there, didn't see, weren't apprised.

Your ears missed inflection, supplied by your friend.
You didn't see gestures, hear words any kind.
It wasn't about you, 'twas nothing you'd done.
Yet speaker's proved wrong in your mind.

So you get an attitude 'gainst one unseen.
Say their "attack" made no sense. Were you there?
Did you see that and hear with own ears?
Or did you take on their offense?

My Word says who judges will be judged, you know.
You've got your plate full with own stuff.
You can't tell Me now you will heft your friend's load
When *your* load's quite more than enough.

Then there's requirement forgive all offenders.
You've not yet forgiven your own.
So how will you work to forgive, make amends
With offenders of friends, though unknown?

Consider effect on your health when you carry,
Remember, rehearse other's pains.
The anger will give you a high for a while
Brings you down, 'cause offender won't change.

How long will you let your friend vent, lay on you
What they don't want for themselves?
You give them relief when you listen, I know.
But without action, offenses fill shelves.

And drawers in your memory
And rooms in your heart.
You've quite a collection in there.
The only way you or your friend will go free
Is to hand all this over in prayer.

Forgiving's the key, letting go of the past,
Trusting I will be judge of all.
So, carry your load and all friends' as well,
Or give it to me. It's your call.

Just remember . . .

     Offenses build fences.

Prisoners of Pride

Lording self o'er others is idolatry and pride
Shows lack and need, holds up to ridicule.
To silence those who see the mask,
Enforcement is required,
So hired guns and tough guys come to rule.

Each layer put in place buys space
To make his lordship higher
And every tier holds those below in pain.
Then soon a tower hearts of stone
Have made for all to see,
But no respect was bought or honor gained.

And this goes on for a space of time
Until the head grows frail,
For every soul shall die eventually.
And meantime, all the stone-heart rats
Are fighting from within, vying for
The place of royalty.

So, when baton of leadership
Has been passed and dust has settled,
Then begins the necessary purge.
Old hearts of stone are massacred;
New hires fight for their place.
Pride beats its chest anew, replacing dirge.

And living at this pinnacle, a lonely figure stands.
There is no trust, no love, no charity.
It takes a hardened heart to rule
A tower made of stone,
The one who rules, a prisoner, never free.

And so, you see, pride has reward,
Has recompense for actions:
A space in time when others must bow down.
But pride will never share the glory;
Each man dies alone.
And in the end, pride's puppet looks a clown.

Prisoners of pride do not consider there's a cost.
They only know the need to be respected.
Amassing money, building wealth,
If family they have,
They have to take great measures it's protected.

Consider Solomon, the King Unparalleled in time.
A Godly man, he held respect of nations.
His wealth unmeasured grew anon,
His power exponential, all gifts became
Commensurate with station.

He was a good man, kind to all,
Avenger of the weak.
His wisdom, boundless,
Brought renown from many.

But in the end, unsatisfied,
He turned away from Me . . .

And served the gods his
Wives brought with them—any.

See, pride corrupts unmercifully;
There is no guard against.
For God alone must be enthroned,
Intuitively sensed.

Only I can keep you humble;
Welcome life's small shames.
Make Me King in your lifetime
And o'er your life I'll reign.

Offer praise while you have breath
And tell My works abroad.
Share what I've done, and sing My praise,
The name of Jesus laud.

Pride then will find no purchase
In My voluntary slave
And you will satisfy my Love,
O one Christ died to save.

He set you free from sin and pride,
Was crucified for all.
Sin's debt was paid and you were bade
Redemption from the Fall.

Laid His life down, then took it back
Three days from when He died,
And bought back every one who'd call . . .
The prisoners of pride.

The Easy Lie

Jesus was . . .
. . . just a man
. . . a prophet
. . . a man who lived a long time ago

    Or He is the Son of God

The Bible . . .
. . . was written by men
. . . was inspired
. . . is one of many religious writings
. . . is just another book

    Or it is God's Word

Heaven is . . .
. . . is a myth
. . . is another name for paradise
. . . doesn't exist
. . . is where my grandma is

    Or it is God's throne

Church is . . .
. . . a building
. . . a place for weak people
. . . a place that has too many rules
. . . where you go to be seen as good

Or is it the body of Christ

The way to heaven is . . .
. . . unknown
. . . to live a good life
. . . doing good deeds
. . . just hope for the best

Or it is through Jesus only

Hell is . . .
. . . a myth
. . . what you threaten your kids with
. . . what preachers talk about
. . . the place you leave your money

Or it is real

God is . . .
. . . a myth too
. . . dead
. . . possibly real . . . maybe
. . . angry with men
. . . allows bad things happen

     Or He is Love

Jesus said . . .
. . . I will never leave you nor forsake you.
. . . I am the way, the truth, and the life.
. . . No man cometh to the Father except by Me.
. . . I am come that you might have life.

     And He knows God keeps His Word.

God's Word says . . .
. . . God is a rewarder of those who seek Him.
. . . There is none holy as the Lord.
. . . Them that honor Me I will honor.

Don't be a sucker.

     Don't fall for the easy lie.

Keep it Jesus

Worship from your heart.
Worship in Spirit and in truth.
Bring to the service true worship
Freely offered to Me, focused on Me,
Telling Me of your love,
And longing to know Me.

All you are looking for in worship,
All your longing, all your thanks,
All your deepest offerings in song,
Bring to Me, and . . . keep it Jesus.

Give Me your truth
Your longing, your sorrow
And your repentance
And I will give you joy to take away regret.

I will remove unworthiness
And replace it with joy,
Giving you a clear consciousness
And hope for tomorrow . . .
    And tomorrow . . . and tomorrow . . .
       And every tomorrow after

Trust Me, child.
I have never forsaken you
And I never will.
           Jesus

The Last Page

The Last Page

What will it be like when
The past page is written?
What will the world be
When the last page is done?

Who will be pointing
The way to the cross then?
Who'll stand to greet You
In Eternity come?

Your Word says we cry out
For the rocks to fall on us
All who've denied You
Will know the truth then.

We'll want to fix it
When it's just too late,
The last page is written
For the souls of all men.

No one is worried now;
Each day the sun shines.
Life seems just limitless;
Tomorrows always come.

We are so busy now;
there's plenty of time.
Who tells the Good News
Of Jesus, God's Son?

Every day there's more of us,
Even though we die.
Never enough laborers
In the harvest of souls.

When the last page
Of Your Word is done, then what?
Will we have accomplished
Any of Your goals?

Will there be disciples?
Those who learn of You?
Men and women willing
To die for Gospel Truth?

Will we go forth singing
"Onward Christian Soldiers"
When it means our lives
Are forfeit to some brute?

Will we have the courage
To say to anyone:
Jesus Christ died for your sins;
You can be born again.

Will we tremble, save ourselves,
And hide out in the darkness?
Or be like Paul,
Proclaim Messiah's come?

What then?

Lord, lead my feet and use my tongue
To talk about the Gospel.
Not witness as a statue cold,
But talk with animation

To tell the God News: Jesus Saves
On cross He triumphed over death
For every tribe and nation.

Today could be the last few hours
Of life I live on Earth
When I open mouth,
Will I strive to be a sage?

Or will I ask
"Do you know Christ?
God's Son who died for you?"

How many can I tell today?

This may be our last page . . .